MERSEYSIDE BUSES
2010–2020

SIMON ACKERS

AMBERLEY

First published 2022

Amberley Publishing
The Hill, Stroud
Gloucestershire, GL5 4EP

www.amberley-books.com

Copyright © Simon Ackers, 2022

The right of Simon Ackers to be identified as
the Author of this work has been asserted in
accordance with the Copyrights, Designs and
Patents Act 1988.

ISBN 978 1 3981 0940 7 (print)
ISBN 978 1 3981 0941 4 (ebook)

British Library Cataloguing in Publication Data.
A catalogue record for this book is available from
the British Library.

Origination by Amberley Publishing.
Printed in the UK.

Introduction

For as long as I can remember I've had an interest in buses. I was five years old when deregulation happened in 1986, at an age where I was oblivious to what the 1985 Transport Act was unleashing on the streets of Merseyside, but intrigued at the array of operator liveries and vehicle types that began to appear over the coming months and years. To this day I still hold a fondness (some may say obsession) for anything Fareway, and while to many 'a bus is a bus', you're nearly always guaranteed to get a reaction from someone when they see a picture of the bus they used to get to school, to town on a Saturday, or the one that went past their nan's house.

A lot has changed on the Merseyside bus network over the years, and it wasn't until I began the detailed work of shortlisting and compiling the content for this book that I realised just how much had taken place over the last decade or so. In 2010 the Arriva Merseyside fleet was still quite strongly made up of ex-MTL vehicles and Stagecoach's of the better-quality remnants of CMT/Glenvale. Jump forward to 2020, and all that remained in that respect was a driver trainer for each. But what else has happened in the timeframe of this book?

First sold their Wirral operations to Stagecoach and other operators have come and gone: Ace Travel, Supertravel, Impera, Strawberry, Napier, Avon and Halton Transport. Fleet profiles have changed: DDA requirements saw all service vehicles becoming low floor, and the big two operators took delivery of new double-deck vehicles in significant numbers to replace single decks. Hybrid and zero-emission vehicles entered service in batches from 2012 as part of the drive to modernise fleets, reduce emissions, and encourage passenger growth. The network has also changed. There are routes still operating the same way that the trams did, but, like some of the operators, some routes across Merseyside were unable to survive declining patronage and increasing operating costs, as well as Merseytravel's supported bus budget being reduced by over £8 million.

Another significant event was the creation of the Liverpool City Region Bus Alliance, formally signed in September 2016 between Merseytravel, Arriva and Stagecoach. One of the most notable successes was the 16 per cent increase in fare-paying passengers, which in the main was as a result of reduced travel costs for those under eighteen. Encouraging people to use public transport at an age where they could be learning to drive at the earliest opportunity can have longer term benefits. The Alliance also saw a commitment to invest, and a number of those vehicles are pictured in this book.

And then there was Covid-19. The effects of coronavirus were undoubtedly wide-reaching and impactful, but in an industry that had long struggled to encourage and grow passenger numbers the implementation of the first national lockdown saw patronage on Merseyside drop down to 10 per cent almost overnight. People were initially encouraged to not use public transport, but then as restrictions were relaxed slowly passengers began to return, and despite many people working from home, reduced capacities, and general public uncertainty, there were week-on-week improvements and some routes recovered better than others depending on the places they served.

It would be impossible to cover every operator, vehicle type, and it took great restraint not to fill the first half of the book with pictures of ex-MTL B10Bs and Olympians. What I hope this book does provide is a colourful journey reflecting what passengers and enthusiasts have experienced on Merseyside, and an opportunity for those from further afield to see the variety offered by Merseyside buses from 2010 up to, and including, 2020.

2224 was part of the batch of new Plaxton Pointer 2-bodied Dennis Darts purchased by Arriva in 2000 following their acquisition of MTL and the need to invest in and modernise the fleet. Route 53 was one that Arriva had competed on with MTL, and then later with Stagecoach. It would become a Quality Partnership Route in July 2011 with a co-ordinated timetable and inter-availability of ticketing.

Pictured departing Queen Square bus station for Kirkby in 2010, P456 DCW was new to Express Travel, Speke, in 1997 and then with UK North, Manchester. It became a Stagecoach bus through their purchase of Glenvale Transport and was renumbered to 33145.

The trademark 'W' frontage of a Wrights-bodied bus has been a familiar sight across the whole of Merseyside for twenty-five years. Scanias were very much the single-deck chassis of choice at First's Rock Ferry depot in the final years before the sale to Stagecoach, and turning into Birkenhead bus station is 60209, a Wrights Axcess Floline-bodied example.

Arriva also had a variety of different bodied Scanias, both step entrance and accessible types. 1058 was a step entrance Northern Counties Paladin example, new in the North Western days and then allocated to St Helens depot.

Peoplesbus Wright Endurance-bodied Volvo B10B 0712, seen here with cherished registration N80 BUS, began life as N659 EKD, new to CMT Buses before being acquired by Glenvale Transport and then moving to Stagecoach Yorkshire.

One of Huyton Travel's commercial ventures was on the 75A; short workings on the 75 route between Liverpool city centre and Liverpool Hope University, on which ex-London Plaxton Pointer-bodied Dennis Dart J139 DUV ran back and forth.

Along with some Volvo B10Bs, the East Lancs Myllenium-bodied DAF SB220, of which 2458 was one, was the higher capacity 'new bus' purchased by Arriva in 2000 to complement the Darts and Cadets. Speke depot had a batch that rarely waivered from route 81 in their fifteen years of service, and the Birkenhead batch were similar on the 410 route between New Brighton and Clatterbridge Hospital.

In a similar way to Arriva, Stagecoach invested in their inherited Glenvale fleet by bringing in new Plaxton Pointer 2-bodied Dennis Darts to replace Titans and step entrance Darts. 34787 is pictured on London Road on route 17 to, as it was then named, Fazakerley Hospital. It later transferred to Stagecoach West.

Quite a rare example, 2401 was one of three Plaxton Prestige-bodied DAF SB220s, new to Arriva London (Leaside), that transferred to Merseyside in December 2000 and was converted to single door operation. It was withdrawn in 2012, and is seen here in September 2010 heading out of Liverpool city centre with St George's Hall as an impressive backdrop.

5303, a Wrights Axcess Ultralow-bodied Scania L113, is pictured on Dale Street in Liverpool city centre. New to Gillmoss depot in 1996, when Arriva had to sell the depot following their takeover of MTL it transferred to Green Lane along with the 12/13 route, where it remained until withdrawal.

Following on from the new Dennis Darts, Stagecoach took delivery of some larger capacity single-deckers in late 2009/early 2010. Forty-five Enviro 300-bodied MANs arrived at Gillmoss, including 24163 that received branding for routes 20/21. It transferred to Hull in 2016, displaced by new double-deckers.

In 2008 Arriva began to take delivery of a large number of Wright Pulsar-bodied VDL SB200s to replace the remaining full-sized step entrance single-decker vehicles and the older low floor examples. 2693 was new in that year and allocated to St Helens, and is seen arriving in the town centre on cross-town route 32A.

Loading in Liverpool ONE bus station, 4113 is an ALX400-bodied Volvo B7, one of thirty delivered in 2006 to Speke depot. These were the first new low floor double-deckers for Arriva Merseyside and operated on routes 82 and 86. Displaced by new Enviro 400s in 2014, the B7s then moved allocation to the 81 route, increasing capacity and replacing the Mylennium DAFs.

Arriva's first Enviro 400-bodied buses had arrived in early 2009 with twenty-three Dennis Trident 2s going to Birkenhead's Laird Street depot for the Cross River routes. 4406 is arriving in Liverpool city centre from West Kirby painted in what would go on to become the standard Arriva livery. As well as the exterior branding, the interior specification saw leather seats with 'cross river' stitched into headrests.

Following on from the Cross River Enviro 400s, Bootle depot received twelve later in 2009 for route 60. 4424 is seen arriving at Bootle bus station with the destination already changed for the return journey to Aigburth. Unlike the Birkenhead examples, these were delivered in standard livery and with standard interiors.

A group of ex-MTL Volvos are pictured on a Sunday morning at the ex-Liverline yard in Bootle, sadly with not long of their operational lives remaining. Until 2013 Bootle depot operated across two sites on Hawthorne Road.

Every few years there tends to be some unexpected or undealt with heavy snow. So bad were the roads around Croxteth Park when the snow came in 2010 service 18A (now just 18) was unable to serve its usual terminus, with Pulsar 2s 3060 and 2958 in contrasting liveries waiting their time over a mile away having turned at the Dwerryhouse Lane roundabout.

At one point as familiar a sight on the streets of Merseyside as the Pulsars became, Wright Endurance-bodied Volvo B10B 6585 is pictured arriving in Liverpool city centre while allocated to Green Lane depot. It was acquired by Lloyds of Machynlleth for spares after withdrawal in 2012.

On 1 January 2011 in Gillmoss depot, 16442 was one of the Northern Counties-bodied Volvo Olympians that had arrived in 2009 from Stagecoach West (Cheltenham & Gloucester), the first double-deckers in the Stagecoach Merseyside fleet. Originally new to Selkent, London, this particular bus went on to operate for Ellie Rose and Abbey Travel.

A batch of Alexander ALX300-bodied DAF SB220s transferred to Arriva Merseyside from Arriva Manchester. Initially at Green Lane for route 14, when the Palatine II-bodied Olympians were retained some moved to Speke. 2407 is pictured in 2011 on the 86B, a variation of the 86 route that would soon be withdrawn as part of the Quality Partnership Agreement introduced in October of that year.

The Plaxton Beaver was a relatively rare sight in Liverpool city centre, but A1A Travel of Birkenhead used T111 JBA on route 107, a previously contracted service that they had taken on commercially.

Stagecoach's MagicBus came to Merseyside in September 2008 and used Volvo B10Ms. A lack of capacity at Queen Square bus station saw the 14C route using Elliot Street for the city centre terminus, the opposite side of St John's Shopping Precinct from the main 14 corridor. The low fare option was withdrawn when the 14 became Merseyside's first Quality Partnership route in January 2011, four days after this photo was taken.

Another pre-Quality Partnership shot, this time for the 10/10A corridor, shows a 10, 10A and 10B on a busy Victoria Street in January 2011, with the Stagecoach Dart and Arriva Pulsar charging to Queen Square bus station on their outbound journeys while the Stagecoach B10B lays over.

Despite the arrival of the Enviro 400s in 2009, the displaced Volvo Olympians still found some use on the Cross River services, although the end was fast approaching. 3303 takes layover on Cook Street in Liverpool city centre, adorning a partial wrap around advert campaign for 'start your own fuel protest'. It was scrapped in 2012 after serving with Blakewater Coaches.

Arriva and First's contrasting Cross River offers are seen side by side on Crosshall Street, Liverpool city centre, in February 2011.

East Lancs Lolyne-bodied Dennis Trident V414 KMY was new to Metrobus (Go-Ahead) London in 1999 and acquired by Maghull Coaches in May 2006. It is pictured here between private hire and school duties in Liverpool city centre.

33179 was a Plaxton Pointer-bodied Dennis Dart, new to CMT Buses and inherited via Glenvale Transport, seen here in 2011 operating the annual shuttle service between Liverpool city centre and Aintree Racecourse during the Grand National event.

Arriva's Liverpool to Southport offering in 2011 was the 47 and 48A, giving a co-ordinated four buses per hour and using route branded Pulsars, of which 3040 was one.

The Stagecoach offering on the Liverpool to Southport corridor was the 38-mile-long X2 that continued on to Preston, operated by route branded Enviro 400-bodied Scanias. The replacement buses that came in 2017 can be seen on page 68.

In 2011 Cumfybus won the Merseytravel contracts for the Liverpool City Centre Circular network of routes. Their successful bid included the commitment to introduce hybrid buses, and ahead of their arrival the routes were operated with conventional Optare Solos. YJ59 PKD is pictured outside Merseytravel's previous headquarters on Hatton Garden.

Above and below are the standard vehicles used on the 10A route between Liverpool and St Helens when it became the latest Quality Partnership route: for Arriva Wright Pulsar-bodied VDL SB200s and for Stagecoach Alexander Dennis Enviro 300 integrals.

Supertravel ran mainly contracted work, of which the 130 was an evenings and Sundays operation on behalf of Merseytravel. The Halton Council contract C1/C1A Runcorn Circular branded Optare Solo is seen mid-route in Liverpool ONE bus station.

The 139 was a new Merseytravel contracted route introduced in 2008 as an amalgamation of two withdrawn commercial services. Cumfybus won the tender and operated it with East Lancs Myllenium-bodied DAF SB220s. C4 MFY was one of eight acquired from London Central, having been new in 1999 for the M1/M2 routes serving the newly opened Millennium Dome.

Plaxton President-bodied Dennis Trident 4002 was new to Blue Bus, Bolton, and retained in the Arriva fleet following their acquisition. Seen here freshly painted and while allocated to Birkenhead depot in 2011, it is loading for a return trip to New Brighton. 4002 was sold to Wigan Coachways in 2015.

ALX400-bodied Transbus Trident X10 BUS (LV52HHX) was new to Stagecoach East London and seen here on Sir Thomas Street in Liverpool city centre on route 52A. For a time Peoplesbus utilised vehicles around contracted school journeys operating commercial journeys on the Liverpool to Netherton route in competition with Arriva.

Huyton Travel invested in a number of new Optare Solos from 2011 to improve the reliability of the fleet. YJ11 EKL was one of those, and is seen here in June of that year arriving at Liverpool South Parkway on route 84. This was a seasonal service that ran for several summers to improve access by public transport to Speke Hall.

Arriva 2434 is pictured at Liverpool South Parkway. New in 2001, this batch of Wright Cadet-bodied DAF SB120s entered service on the 75 route, but struggled with capacity (a fact I can vouch for having had to use them at university) so were moved onto the 80/80A where they spent the remainder of their fifteen years.

The 500 route between Liverpool city centre and Liverpool John Lennon Airport has long been a high profile one. For nearly seven years Arriva operated three Scania Omnicitys in Airlink livery. 2063 is arriving at Liverpool ONE bus station in 2011. The trio transferred to Arriva North East the year after.

The 501 was a short rail-air link between Liverpool South Parkway and Liverpool John Lennon Airport. The route was initially operated by Airlink liveried and branded Wright Commander-bodied VDL SB200s, as shown on 2602.

The 501 was never a highly patronised route, but in the summer of 2011 the available capacity was increased when Arriva had to find a use for the London exodus of articulated buses. The Mercedes-Benz Citaros suited the principle of the route, even if the 149 capacity proved a little luxurious. If you look closely at this picture of 6005 you can actually see a passenger!

A very rare bus type on Merseyside was this BMC Falcon with Ace Travel in September 2011, out of service heading to start peak time route 103. It was sold not long after being photographed and later came back to Merseyside for a time with Al's Coaches. In the background is the former railway bridge above the double roundabout at Broadway.

Another ex-CMT/Glenvale vehicle that remained in service with Stagecoach until withdrawal in 2014 was 21111, a Wright Renown-bodied Volvo B10B.

Scania L113 5305 is pictured travelling through Queen Square bus station in 2011, shortly before the end of its operational life, on route 12, the route it was bought new for in 1996.

DK57 OPZ, new in 2007, gave some higher capacity for Huyton Travel on their busier commercial services. It is seen here at Liverpool South Parkway on the 188 Garston–Belle Vale Circular.

Cumfybus Optare Solo YJ59 PKD is parked outside George's Dock Building, Liverpool city centre.

Stagecoach 33029 was an ex-Hong Kong Dennis Dart that spent time on Merseyside in 2011, seen here at the Penny Lane bus terminus when Stagecoach took their turn at trying to make a success of route 107/207 after A1A Travel had stopped operating.

Arriva 4096 was an ALX400-bodied DAF DB250, new to Arriva London Northern in 1999. It was one of the many buses that would be transferred up from London and converted to single door operation, and is seen here arriving in Liverpool city centre, soon to depart back across to Wirral.

Having traditionally operated on the eastern side of the River Mersey, Supertavel expanded in 2011 when they won a number of Wirral-based Merseytravel contracts, however their operating base remained in Hunts Cross. Streetlite MX11 EGE was one of the new buses for the extra work, due to depart on the Newton and West Kirby Circular 138 route. Later that year Supertravel ceased trading.

When the Cross River Arriva Hybrids arrived in 2013 the batch of Enviro 400s were split, with twelve transferring to Bootle depot for route 61 and nine going to Chester depot to be converted to Arriva Sapphire spec for route 1 Wrexham to Chester. 4402, here at West Kirby Station, was one of the latter. It subsequently also moved to Winsford but retained the Arriva Wales number plate J200 ABW.

Avon had eleven MCV Evolution-bodied ADL Enviro 200s and AE07 DZS was one of the shorter 8.9-metre examples, waiting at West Kirby station to commence the return trip to Birkenhead via Heswall.

First's Rock Ferry depot had a number of ex-Capital Citybus Alexander RH-bodied Volvo Olympians still with their centre doors. Although predominantly used on schools they did frequently find their way to general services too.

P548 EFL, a Northern Counties-bodied Volvo Olympian, was another Rock Ferry double-decker primarily used on schools and the 38 route. Though pictured here when with First, it was actually with Stagecoach on two occasions either side of this. It had gone to First Manchester after returning off lease, and was then reacquired by Stagecoach when they purchased Rock Ferry and Chester depots.

Alexander Royale-bodied Volvo Olympian 30803, here loading in Birkenhead bus station, was new in 1997 in Yorkshire and moved to Rock Ferry in 2008. It was withdrawn in 2013 after having transferred to Manchester.

In summer 2011 Olympian 3295 was still carrying branding for and operating on Cross River routes, seen here on the 464 in Birkenhead bus station. It soon went on to operate with Decker Bus and with Shoreys Travel.

Another type of Scania new to North Western was a batch of East Lancs Flyte-bodied examples, of which 1040 was one. It spent many a year operating out of St Helens, but in the final few months it had been transferred to Speke depot and is pictured on Brownlow Hill on the 78.

Ace Travel had this ex-Bus Eireann Plaxton Pointer-bodied Dennis Dart, parked here at the Pier Head on driver shuttle duties for the sightseeing buses. It later went to operate with Lloyds of Machynlleth.

Nearly thirty more Arriva Pulsar 2s were delivered to Arriva Merseyside in 2011. 3083 is pictured at a promotional event in September of that year when brand new. Although allocated to Southport depot, the location is Liverpool ONE shopping centre.

2011 also saw Arriva take delivery of forty-four new Wright Gemini 2-bodied VDL DB300s for Speke depot, split between routes 79 and 82. 4478 is arriving at Liverpool ONE bus station from Hanover Street.

New to Arriva Cymru in 1998, 3344 spent the final operational years of life having transferred to Merseyside to be with other Volvo Olympians. In September 2011 it is allocated to Bootle depot and on route 56.

When photographed in front of the now deconstructed Churchill Way Flyover former MTL 'Millennium Fleet' Volvo Olympian 3313 still had eighteen months or so of service left with Arriva. By this stage those that remained kept getting pushed from route to route as newer buses arrived, and were transferred around the fleet to cover where required.

Originally with London Central and then Go North East, Avon had T423 AGP, one of two short Marshall-bodied Dennis Darts, here loading in Birkenhead bus station.

Arriva Merseyside withdrew the last step entrance Volvo B10B in late 2011. Sad on a personal level but they had served Merseyside well in their fifteen plus years, with many going on to operate elsewhere. 6599 is pictured turning in front of Number 1 Mann Island, the under-construction head offices for Merseytravel and later the Combined Authority.

AlX400-bodied Dennis Trident 17272, operating with cherished plate HSV 194, was new to Selkent in 2000 as X272 NNO. It was part of the introduction of low floor double-deckers to the Gillmoss fleet in 2011, leaving five years later in 2016 when it transferred to Chester to operate school contracts. The cherished number plate of HSV 194 was reassigned to a Stagecoach Gold Optare Solo later that year.

Between September 2012 and April 2013 James Street Merseyrail station was closed as part of a multimillion-pound refurbishment. A replacement bus service was operated for the duration of the closure, with Selwyns operating some of Abellio's London Tridents on a circular route around Liverpool city centre.

821 was one of a pair of East Lancs Spryte-bodied Dennis Darts new to Avon in 2000. Here it is departing on Merseyravel's contracted 492 service from Woodside bus station at a point before the infrastructure was removed.

Another Peoplebus ALX400-bodied Transbus Trident LV52 HHC is seen here at the 2012 Wirral Bus & Tram Show showing off the new livery.

A2B Travel operated a mixture of private hire and Merseytravel contract work, primarily using Optare Solos on the latter. YJ60 KFA is pictured at New Brighton in January 2013.

In 2013 First completed the sale of their Rock Ferry and Chester depots to Stagecoach for £4.5 million, with 100 vehicles becoming part of Stagecoach Merseyside & South Lancashire. Wright Eclipse-bodied Volvo B7 32453 was renumbered to 16960 and is seen here on Woodchurch Road in January 2013 in First livery with Stagecoach logos.

It had been a number of years since there had been any real fleet investment by First at Rock Ferry, and Stagecoach moved quickly to address that by diverting the arrival of new integral Alexander Dennis Enviro 300s intended for Gillmoss. 36811 is passing through the same junction as 16960.

Arriva 2451 was new to Laird Street depot, but the arrival of Pulsars for the 410 route saw it transfer to Speke depot as the type reached the stage in their operational life where they became spare buses and their allocation varied.

Impera were a new independent start-up company based on the Wirral. They operated a mixture of Merseytravel supported general and schools contracts, as well as commercial routes. Y675 NLO 'Tabitha Theresa' was a Plaxton Pointer-bodied Dennis Dart new to Metroline, London, and is photographed here on one of those commercial journeys at Woodside with the Ferry terminal in the background. The bus later became a mobile catering unit.

The first batch of hybrid buses operating on Merseyside arrived in 2012 in the form of thirteen Optare Solos purchased by Cumfybus with a £1.2-million grant from the Green Bus Fund. YJ12 GXA is seen here turning from James Street onto Castle Street on one of the city centre circular routes.

In May 2013 two of the Wright Gemini 2 buses are pictured at the Speke Morrisons terminus. The facility was a much improved offering from the square of road space previously used as the bus terminus for the area. 4478 is arriving, while 4475 is preparing to depart.

The original intended use for Arriva's ex-London Citaros were routes 26/27, but as well as the 501 they found a home on the 699 university service. 6005 is seen on Smithdown Road in 2013.

Here we see a nearside view of one of the articulated offerings on the university link service.

3313 makes its second appearance, still in service in March 2013 but having transferred to Speke depot and received an electronic destination display. When withdrawn by Arriva, it passed to Peoplesbus for Greenbus school operations.

24134, one of the Stagecoach MANs route branded for the 14, is seen here on Canada Boulevard in front of the Pier Head's Three Graces.

Between the withdrawal of the Scania L113s and the arrival of the Enviro 400s the 12/13 Liverpool to Stockbridge Village routes experienced a varied vehicle allocation. Plaxton Pointer-bodied Dennis Dart 2216 is waiting to turn out of West Derby Village in March 2013.

Another example of the varied allocation is one of the ex-Arriva Manchester DAFs, with 2414 seen here in Stockbridge Village.

Wright Solar-bodied Scania L94UB 65740 was renumbered to 28552 in the Stagecoach fleet and is seen here on Sir Thomas Street in Liverpool city centre in First livery with Stagecoach logos. Later repainted into Stagecoach livery and eventually withdrawn in 2017, this particular vehicle was then sold to Connexions Buses operated by Harrogate Coach Travel.

A slightly older example than 28552 but in the same location, 21250 shows the application of the Stagecoach livery.

In March 2013 thirty-three new electric hybrid buses arrived at Laird Street depot for the Cross River services. The Wright Eclipse Gemini 2-bodied Volvo B5LHs were painted in Arriva's corporate hybrid livery with Cross River branding applied. Their arrival displaced the Enviro 400s to Bootle and Chester, and a further seven hybrids transferred in from Manchester at a later date.

Stagecoach also brought in 'new' buses to their cross river 471/472 route, replacing the Eclipse-bodied B7s with Alexander Dennis Enviro 400s from Stagecoach Manchester. 19054 was replaced on the route in late 2017 by the Gold Enviro 400 MMCs and then transferred to Fife in May 2019.

V660 LWT was a rare UVG Urbanstar-bodied Dennis Dart new to Hatton's in 1999 and saw sixteen years' service before being sold in 2014 and finding its way to Glastonbury as a 'magic bus'. It's seen here arriving in St Helens town centre in April 2013.

ALX400-bodied Volvo B7 4111 is pictured departing Queen Square bus station for Halewood.

Impera continued to expand their commercial network into Cross River provision, creating and reinstating previously lost links such as the 98 that gave the Beechwood and Noctorum estates a direct bus to Liverpool. Ex-Go-Ahead Plaxton Pointer-bodied Dennis Dart S374 ONL is seen departing Liverpool city centre for Moreton in May 2013. Impera ceased trading later that year in October.

Cumfybus Optare Solo YN04 LXC is waiting time at Aintree station interchange in May 2013, operating what was then one of their commercial services between Bootle and Aintree.

In July 2012 fifteen Optare Solo Slimlines came to Arriva St Helens depot for service on local routes. 715 is pictured in Church Square in April 2013 preparing for an engagement event.

The 89 route between St Helens and Liverpool John Lennon Airport was one that had been subject to kickstart funding and grown into a regular all day service. Wright Renown-bodied Volvo B10BLE 2706 is seen, contrary to the destination blind, arriving in St Helens town centre with what remains of the St Helens Rugby League side vinyls.

Huyton Travel have operated Merseytravel's contracted 102 service since 2008. Optare Solo YJ11 EXP travels through the Croxteth Hall Estate en route to one of the three hospitals the route links.

Electronic destination blinds allowed a flexibility of what could be displayed for passengers. It became standard spec for a time for Merseytravel contracts to show 'Merseytravel Supported Service' scrolling beneath the static destination. Here the 130, one of the first to show it, waits in Mann Island to depart its first evening trip. MX12 CFK was a leased vehicle that returned to the dealer when Ace Travel ceased operating in 2015.

In 2013 Merseytravel received LSTF (Local Sustainable Transport Funding) monies for a network of industrial type services to improve access to the Jaguar Land Rover Factory in Halewood, running at bespoke times in line with shift start and finish times. Gemini 2 4470 waits to depart the afternoon J5 journey to Kirkby in May of that year.

As part of the Quality Bus Partnership on route 14 between Liverpool city centre and Croxteth both Arriva and Stagecoach invested in new vehicles similar to the 10A: VDL SB200s and ADL Enviro 300s respectively. The co-ordinated timetable is not quite co-ordinated in this photo at the former tram terminus at Broadway, Norris Green.

Cumfybus hybrid YJ12 GXH is seen here entering the Albert Dock on the City Link service. The City Link route was a high frequency circular one linking many of Liverpool city centre's tourist and cultural attractions. This particular vehicle was one of the buses that later transferred to Bolton to operate on TfGM contracted services.

For a number of years Avon Buses would take a Merseytravel contracted service, amend it slightly, and operate it commercially, sometimes with some deminimis support for particular sections that provided a base to grow the route and its viability. As such, some of their routes operated in the more rural areas of Wirral, such as this 2013 shot of Plaxton Pointer 2-bodied Dennis Dart 124, previously new to A1A Travel, travelling past the Thornton Manor estate.

Peoplesbus Dennis Dart SLF W869YNB was new to Jim Stones in Leigh, then Northumbria Coaches and Go North East. In 2013 it is pictured in Prescot Bus Station on route 111, a short-lived service introduced with Local Sustainable Transport Funding (LSTF) to improve links between Stockbridge Village and Whiston Hospital. Unfortunately the service was withdrawn when the funding expired.

MV54 AOO was a Wright Merit-bodied VDL SB120 new to Hatton's in 2004. It's seen here arriving in Prescot bus station, a facility now in the shadow of Shakespeare in the North, on their commercial 297 service linking St Helens and Kirkby.

Mann Island in Liverpool city centre has long been a bus terminus, but over the years the number of services terminating here and taking official layover has decreased, partly due to the resource requirements of travelling through the city centre. Despite marked stands for up to six buses, there was always the potential for some imaginative parking when all were occupied. Ex-MTL Marshall-bodied Dennis Dart 7630 is pictured here taking layover on the roundabout.

Although a common bus type, the ADL Enviro 200 is a type that only just breaks into double figures in the Arriva Merseyside fleet. Having operated Sefton Council's Park & Ride contract in Southport for many years (previously with gas-powered buses) four were purchased in 2008 and painted in the old Southport colours. On losing the contract in 2018, the buses were repainted into standard livery and used in general service. A further eight older examples were also transferred from Arriva London.

X662 WCH, an East Lancs-bodied Dennis Trident, was acquired from Nottingham by Cumfybus mainly for school duties. Although showing 781 – a Chesterfield High School route – it is on driver shuttle duties in November 2013.

As some of the photos in this book show, some buses transfer from depot to depot or operate with numerous companies. 7655, however, spent all of its years allocated to Southport depot, and is seen here passing the Monument in the town centre. Like the majority of the batch, it was scrapped after fifteen years rather than be sold on for further service. While remembered fondly by some, my main memory of these is their rattle, even when new!

Peoplesbus Optare Tempo V1 BUS, fleet number 0701, is seen here on Victoria Street, Liverpool city centre, in September 2013. New in 2009 and originally YJ59 GHV, it moved to Tanant Valley Coaches, Shropshire, in 2015.

In early 2014 Cross River Volvo Hybrid 4506 heads a convoy of liveries in Birkenhead bus station. Despite appearances, this side of the bus station is actually public highway.

KU52 YCB was acquired by Avon from Impera when they ceased trading and is seen here in a contrasting shot to the Woodside bus station of page 36. Woodside is quite a shadow of its former self when compared to older photos and memories where the number of buses lined up was quite staggering.

As some of the Cumfybus Hybrids moved to Manchester for newly won contracts, the City Link contract became operated by branded Solo SRs. The branding was linked to a marketing campaign to try and appeal to tourists and local commuters.

On 1 September 2014 the first batch of Arriva's integral ADL Enviro 400s entered service. 4560 was one of the nineteen allocated to Speke depot for routes 86/86A, operating between Liverpool city centre and Garston/Liverpool John Lennon Airport. 128 Enviro 400s would be delivered between September 2014 and June 2015, significantly enhancing the capacity on offer compared to the volume of single-deck buses ten years earlier.

Stagecoach also had new arrivals in 2014. In October fourteen ADL Enviro 300s entered service at Gillmoss for service 17. 27148 is pictured on Castle Street in Liverpool city centre.

Arriva 2633, a Wright Cadet-bodied VDL SB120, turns in Liverpool ONE bus station on service 76, a former Merseytravel tendered route that was grown into a commercial one. It never made it to high frequency but formed an integral part of Arriva's Halewood network.

As part of redevelopment works on the Merseyrail network, Hamilton Square station in Birkenhead was closed from the autumn of 2014 to the spring of 2015. Stagecoach operated the rail replacement service out of their Rock Ferry depot with some ex-London Dennis Tridents. LV52 HFH went on to become an open-top tour bus in Stratford with Stagecoach Midlands.

Halton Transport took delivery of twelve MCV Evolution-bodied Alexander Dennis Enviro 200s between 2007 and 2009. Fleet number 12 is pulling into Queen Square bus station in 2015 to begin the near two-hour trip to Runcorn.

January 2015 saw the next batch of Arriva's new Enviro 400s enter service, with thirty-six split between Green Lane (for the 10B) and St Helens (for the 10/10A) depots. 4584 is in Queen Square bus station and carrying promotional advertising.

A further fifteen Enviro 400s arrived in March 2015, this time for Bootle depot's 52/52A. 4635 is pictured on Sir Thomas Street when new in service before any advertising had been applied.

The first Enviro 400MMC came to Merseyside in May 2015 when Stagecoach took demonstrator 80027, with stop start technology, seen here on the X3 in Liverpool city centre. After a short time it moved to Manchester and was renumbered 10430 in 2017. Note the slightly different livery and fleet number application on the front in comparison to the standard examples that would arrive later.

Over the years Al's Coaches took a number of ex-Dublin Olympians, and two are seen here on The Strand in Liverpool city centre in their contrasting liveries.

The versatility of electronic destination blinds does not just lend itself to route vias and advertising. Enviro 400 4613 shows 'Remember the 96' reflecting on the Hillsborough disaster.

In 2015 six Wrightbus Streetlites arrived at Laird Street depot for route 487 and received Cross River branding. Although in standard fleet livery, they were fitted with micro hybrid technology; this recovers energy lost from braking to power the vehicle electrics and compressed air systems. 4006 is seen here travelling through the village of Thornton Hough from Ness Gardens.

The 17 between St Helens and Widnes became a Quality Partnership route between Arriva, Halton Transport, Merseytravel, St Helens Council and Halton Council in 2015. The vehicle allocation varied, but in May 2016 Alexander Dennis Enviro 200 DK60 AHO is laying over in St Helens town centre.

Hatton's Scania Omnicity YN54 NXL was new to Nottingham in 2004. It's seen here parked on Corporation Street in St Helens town centre being used for driver breaks in-between school duties.

The A10 was a short-lived replacement for one of the Eco Bus routes that used to operate around the town centre of St Helens, and its short distance allowed it to be interworked with Merseytravel routes 137/138. One of Huyton Travel's Solo SRs is pictured in the bus station.

The 138 route was withdrawn in 2016 as part of the St Helens Network Review, a process reviewing the borough's network as a whole with a view to reducing service duplication and align daytime and evening services. A number of links were lost with the withdrawal of the 138; however, faced with a reduced budget for providing supported bus services, all areas of St Helens remained within 400 metres of a bus service Monday to Saturday daytimes.

MX55 YBA was new to Hatton's in 2006 and is seen here leaving St Helens town centre for Bold on their commercial 140 route. The service had originally been a Merseytravel contract, that became commercial and remained so for a number of years. Unfortunately gradual passenger decline and competition on certain sections with more frequent routes led to it being withdrawn in 2019.

Optare Solo 680 was originally new to Arriva Manchester before transferring to St Helens. A lack of designated layover in and around St Helens bus station means finding a space wherever you can!

The lack of layover is encapsulated in this shot of Bickerstaffe Street, with Pulsar 2939 parked on a departure stop, 2972 in the inside running lane with hazard lights on, and B10BLE 2705 heading round to enter the bus station.

As well as operating buses Hatton's were also a well-established coach operator. Running local services gave an excellent opportunity to advertise, as can be seen on the side of this Enviro 200.

Stagecoach's first batch of ADL Enviro 400 MMCs arrived in May 2016 for routes 14, 82 and 86. These replaced single-deck vehicles, so brought some further capacity to the busier routes. 10548 is laying over at the Mann Island terminus when only a couple of weeks old.

In December 2016 Arriva's new hybrid double-deckers began to arrive: twenty-six for Green Lane routes 14 and 18, and twenty-four for Speke depot. They were Wright Gemini 3-bodied Volvo H5TLs, and continued the improvements in fleet emissions and capacity. 4800 and 4802 are parked here at their launch at Mann Island. Before entering normal service they first covered the Merseyrail City Centre loop shuttle. As a daily user of the 18, I was very happy with these replacing Pulsars!

Enviro 400-bodied Dennis Trident 2 19018 has operated out of many depots in both England and Scotland, and for a time was allocated to Rock Ferry. In this shot it is in the Gillmoss workshop undergoing some of the unseen and often unappreciated maintenance that is required to keep vehicles on the road.

Having already introduced over fifty hybrid vehicles and nine gas-powered vehicles, at the end of 2017 twelve fully electric BYD ADL Enviro 200EVs were delivered to Arriva's Green Lane depot for use on service 26/27. Covering 130 miles on a single charge, they also met what had become the 'standard' Merseyside Bus Alliance specification of leather seats, free Wi-Fi, and USB charging.

As well as the twelve BYD electrics there were nineteen MAN Gas EcoCitys for Runcorn depot, photographed at the Bus Alliance promotional launch in September 2017.

In November 2017 Stagecoach launched their own new arrivals: eighteen Alexander Dennis Enviro 400MMCs. Seven were for Rock Ferry to Gold specification for the 471/472 and eleven for Preston for the X2. The latter were in standard livery but did have luxury interiors including tables.

Having entered service, 10882 is seen here in Cook Street, Liverpool city centre, with a couple of Arriva Cross Rivers on the layover stand behind.

Halton Transport took six 11.3-metre Marshall Capital 2-bodied Dennis Darts in 2002. Fleet number 29 is laying over on Dale Street in Liverpool city centre in March 2018.

Avon's 'new' livery is seen here on MCV Evolution-bodied 9.3-metre Dennis Dart parked in their Prenton depot. Alongside it is Volvo B10M M420 RRN, an ex-driver trainer that left East Yorkshire Motor Services in June 2016.

Pictured in January 2018, Y174 NLK, a Plaxton President-bodied Volvo B7 previously of Metroline and Go Whippet, was one of the double-deckers that Avon took when they began operating commercial school journeys, quite a change from what had long been a wholly single-decker fleet.

In August 2018 Volvo, Stagecoach, and Merseytravel partnered on a two-month trial of a fully electric Volvo 7900E bus. The difference between this and those in service with Arriva was that this charged via an inverted pantograph installed in the Liverpool ONE bus station layover area.

As well as the old Widnes Corporation depot, Halton Transport had an extra yard just around the corner to provide additional parking space. A selection of East Lancs-bodied Darts and Scania Omnicitys are on view one Sunday afternoon.

In autumn 2018 another seventeen Enviro 400MMCs arrived at Gillmoss. 11114 is entering Queen Square bus station in January 2019.

In March 2019 a Hydrogen-powered demonstrator came to Mann Island as part of the launch of the Liverpool City Region's Combined Authority's Hydrogen Bus Project. The project was for an initial twenty hydrogen vehicles and a fuelling station, funded directly by the Combined Authority and boosted by the Transforming Cities Fund.

Again in March 2019, Arriva commemorated late local comedian Kenn Dodd with a bus that operated on the 10/10A routes running through his Knotty Ash, and Gemini 2-bodied VDL DB300 4438 was chosen. This had previously carried an all-over livery as part of the Liverpool Biennial Arts Festival.

On a rainy April afternoon, Arriva hybrid 4831 is turning into Queen Square bus station from St George's Place, with Lime Street station in the background.

Transport events are always enjoyable to attend, the range of current and preserved vehicles on show meaning there's something for the most hardcore enthusiast to just being a nice family day out. Pulsar 3030, fresh from the paint shop, was in attendance at the North West Vehicle Trust's annual open/running day in June 2019.

SN06 BMY, an 8.8-metre Plaxton Pointer 2-bodied ADL Dart, was new to Huyton Travel in 2006. It is seen here on service 898 arriving at Knowsley Industrial Park (Kirkby Admin for those over a certain age). The 898 operates hourly between 05.20 and 23.12 maintaining key employment links.

Cumfybus Solo SR YJ13 HNK makes another appearance, this time travelling through Garswood and carrying standard Cumfybus livery having previously been branded for the City Link service (page xx Photo 55).

Despite being one of the oldest vehicles in the Arriva Merseyside fleet, Volvo B7 4103 was repainted into the new livery. Here it is during its allocation to Laird Street depot operating Cross River route 437 on Victoria Street, Liverpool city centre.

While the Enviro 400 MMC is a common sight on Merseyside from a Stagecoach perspective, Arriva has just five. New in 2017 and originally allocated to route 55, 4697 is photographed operating a 60 journey to Aigburth.

One of the original Bootle depot Enviro 400s, 4430 is seen here on Muirhead Avenue on route 62 to Penny Lane. As well as an exterior repaint, the batch also underwent interior refurbishment bringing all 142 to a near standard appearance.

A trio of double-deckers lined up in Bootle depot in August 2019: Plaxton President-bodied DAF SB250 4170, ALX400-bodied Volvo B7 4102, and Enviro 400-bodied Trident 2 4433. I know which one I'd not choose!

Stagecoach Gold first came to Merseyside in 2015 when eighteen Enviro 200s were delivered for routes 1 and 2 between Liverpool and Chester. As well as the free Wi-Fi and USB charging, and hand-stitched Italian-designed leather seats, they were Euro 5 engined and ran off bio diesel. 27255 is pictured in 2019.

BYD electric 7008 is pictured here loading in Liverpool ONE bus station with the Albert Dock in the background.

2019 saw fifty years since the creation of Merseyside Public Transport Executive (M.P.T.E), and to mark the semicentenary Arriva repainted Enviro 400 4590 into the verona green and jonquil livery of the North Division, complete with brown logos, skirt and window surrounds. It moved between Green Lane, St Helens and Speke depots, and is seen here on the Sheil Road Circular 26.

The year 2019 was a key year in local bus history, with it also being the Ribble centenary. Another Enviro 400 was repainted into a special livery, with Bootle allocated 4411 carrying Ribble red with white stripe and the post-1972 logo that showed both the NBC and MPTE logos. Unfortunately I never managed a photo of 4411 on the last remaining Bootle Ribble route (the 58).

Driver training fleets often give some vehicles an extended period of life. Arriva renumber buses that enter the driver training fleet, and 8201 was formerly 6301, one of three Alexander Strider-bodied Volvo B10Bs new to MTL/Merseyrider in 1994, making it twenty-five years old when photographed in August 2019.

Stagecoach painted one of their driver training vehicles into CMT livery, complete with full logos and low-floor branding. W467 CRN, a Wright Renown-bodied Volvo B10BLE was new to CMT in 2000.

One aspect of Liverpool City Council's multimillion Liverpool City Centre Connectivity Scheme was the construction of a 'Bus Hub', a centralised area on Old Haymarket for buses to take layover rather than in designated on-street stands around the city centre. Seen here carrying out the first bus test on the facility in December 2019 is Wright Eclipse Urban-bodied Volvo B7RLE 8254. It was new to KMP Llanberis in 2004 and passed into the Arriva Cymru fleet on their acquisition.

Volvo B10B 8252 was new to St Helens depot, where it spent most of its service life, in 2001 as fleet number 2702. No vans were damaged carrying out this manoeuvre, though a fine example of why computer tracking should always be verified with a bus test!

Enviro 400-bodied Scania 15581, originally new to Preston, represented Stagecoach Gillmoss on the bus test. Alongside it, 8255 was another ex-KMP Llanberis bus, new in 2005 as M7KMP.

Stagecoach Enviro 400-bodied Scania 15588, with cherished plate TSV 722, is pictured in one of the centre layover stands during one of the follow up bus tests in January 2020. It wears an all-over livery supporting the Better By Bus Campaign with the message 'We can't wait to tackle climate change' and a large polar bear on the side.

Taken just a couple of days before Halton Transport ceased trading on 24 January 2020, East Lancs-bodied Dart 41 waits in the rain as the light fades – literally and metaphorically.

Maghull Coaches YN56 FDF, a Scania Omnidekka, awaits the return of school pupils on a trip to the Museum of Liverpool Life. It was one of three purchased via Ensignbus in late 2016, having started life in London with Metrobus (Go-Ahead).

Arriva Click, a new DRT offer, came to Liverpool in 2018 with high spec Mercedes Sprinters. Bookable via an app and taking you to and from where you wanted to go (within the initial South Liverpool operating zone) when you wanted to go it offered something new and different. The flexibility of the vehicles saw it replace the conventional 211 Speke Circular route and also take on shuttle bus contracts. These remained, but the Covid-19 pandemic saw the DRT aspect cease in 2020. RF68 FLL is outside Liverpool Dental Hospital.

Solo passes Solo on Fir Tree Drive, Croxteth Park, with Cumfy's Hybrid YJ12 GXN and HTL's YJ61 MOF on Merseytravel's 215 and 102 routes respectively.

Enviro 400-bodied Scania 15593 transferred to Stagecoach Gillmoss in July 2018 from Stagecoach South. Before being repainted into standard livery it operated for a time with full Coastliner South Coast branding.

By the time 2020 arrived most of the Plaxton Pointer-bodied Darts that Stagecoach had modernised the Glenvale fleet with had been withdrawn, transferred, or put into storage. However, the type remained in single figures, carrying simple branding for the 204 route. 34820 is pictured here at Belle Vale bus station.

The Plaxton Centro-bodied VDL SB120 was represented across six depots in the Arriva North West fleet in 2020, and there were only eleven of the type. 2614 was allocated to Runcorn and is travelling through Liverpool city centre to Queen Square bus station to start its journey.

When the new Hybrid Volvo B5s arrived at Speke in 2016/2017, eleven 2013 Gemini 2-bodied examples transferred in from Arriva Kent & Surrey in 2017. 4859 is pictured on route 81 heading to Bootle bus station. At this point the Covid-19 restrictions on public transport were in place, which saw face coverings being mandatory and change no longer being given. Destination blinds would alternate, with the number constant but the destination changing to the advisory message seen here.

In January 2020 Stagecoach unveiled their change in livery(s), with the well-established swoops replaced with a simplified look based on customer feedback. The new colours for standard services is seen here on MAN 24176 taking layover on Victoria Street, Liverpool city centre.

24179 offers a nearside view of the new livery.

Stagecoach Enviro 400 MMC 10534 wears an all-over Remembrance livery in partnership with the British Legion. It also has cherished plate VKB 708, previously carried by Dart 34820 (pictured earlier on the 204 at Belle Vale) and, even earlier, by Liverpool Corporation Leyland PD2 L252.

10572 is pictured parked in Gillmoss depot in the designated space for buses on routes 14 and 19 carrying out driver changeovers or taking layover. The Willow Way terminus for the 14 is the opposite side of the East Lancs, so this option negates the requirement for a shuttle van. Of an evening the short 14 and 19 journeys interwork so can also take their layover inside the depot without having to travel a circuitous trip around the one-way system.

Between journeys on route 215, Cumfybus Solo MX08 DJE displays the destination display that was programmed to be shown should the bus reach the reduced maximum capacity due to social distancing. During the first lockdown period for this particular bus it would have been single figured.

Three of Arriva's Hybrid Volvo B5s are seen here at Mann Island in September 2020, with the works that would see the road permanently closed off well underway.

DfE funding allowed Merseytravel to duplicate commercial journeys where the reduced social distancing capacities caused an overcrowding problem with the high number of pupils travelling to and from schools. Only school children were allowed on the 'S Buses'. Here an Arriva 18 overtakes the S18 duplicate, with the latter only operating a short journey based on usage so it could then operate a second trip. 18325 was new to Manchester and then served in the Lake District.

Stagecoach 15740 was one of the Enviro 400-bodied Scanias that came to Rock Ferry depot from Stagecoach Midlands in 2018 for the increased PVR on the Liverpool to Chester 1/X1 route but the Covid-19 frequency reductions saw the surplus vehicles used on school resource contracts.

Al's Coaches operated some of the Liverpool school resource journeys, with Scania Omnidekka YT59 DYS pictured in West Derby Village duplicating Arriva's 61A from Bootle to Aigburth. The vehicle is fitted with an unattractive but very much required tree defender on the upper deck front window due to the number of low hanging trees across the Wirral where Al's operate the majority of their school services.

Like Al's, Selwyns operated school services on the Wirral but won some of the to Liverpool-based resource contracts. Alexander Dennis Enviro 400 MMC SN16 OGY is seen here on Muirhead Avenue duplicating the 62 to Penny Lane.

An ex-Stagecoach Midlands and then Chester-based vehicle, 39691 is an Alexander Dennis Enviro 200 waiting to commence an afternoon duplicate of Arriva's 60 to Aigburth Vale. It would then duplicate the return trip back to Bootle. The 60 had the most duplicate journeys on due to the number of schools it covered.

New to Stagecoach Manchester, then at Preston and Gillmoss before moving to Rock Ferry, ALX400-bodied Trident 2 18372 was another used on the school resource boards, waiting time here on Stanley Park Avenue North ahead of commencing an S81 journey.

Cumfybus gained some school contracts from April 2020 that required double-decker capacities, but due to the Covid-19 school closures many didn't enter service until September 2020. Smartly repainted and in their Aintree depot is ex-Preston Bus Hybrid Wright Gemini 2-bodied Volvo B5H PO62 LNF.

Service revisions from 30 August 2020 saw the 79 no longer operate across Liverpool city centre between Queen Square and Liverpool ONE bus stations, with the service instead split to serve either. The Queen Square variant was numbered 79Q. The 79Q was withdrawn in January 2021.

The route of the 19 can be traced back to the days of the tram, operating the near same route from Liverpool city centre to Southdene in Kirkby. 24167 is travelling inbound along Walton Hall Avenue at the Richard Kelly Drive junction, having passed beneath the old loop line bridge of the same structural design as the bridge at Broadway in earlier photos.

Despite the bus tests in January 2020, the 'Bus Hub' layover facility was still not fully in use by October; hence the undisturbed leafy surface in this autumnal shot of 24158 laying over in one of the on-street bays.

Arriva Hybrid 4800 received a mask in October 2020 as part of the promotional work encouraging/reminding people of the requirement to wear a face covering when using public transport.

As part of their corporate fundraising, in 2014 Arriva painted Enviro 400 4426 in an all-over livery promoting Zoe's Place, a hospice that provides palliative, respite and end-of-life care to babies and infants aged from birth to five years suffering from life-limiting or life-threatening conditions, in and around the North West. Here 4426 shows the Christmas 2020 alternating destination display while on service 62 outside Aintree University Hospital.